Don't talk down to me!
6 MONEY BASIC
ADVICE FOR WOMEN

These are the most important financial tips I have learned and would have liked to read as a young woman, and now I find myself sharing this information with other women every time I could.

Ariana C P Hunter

I dedicate this book to my Maker, my daughters and their friends, aunts, and most in importantly my Mother Eliana Vilchez Castillo
My mother who taught me to value work and who still get up to go to work each day.

San Antonio, Texas

Contents

Introduction

Why another financial book for women? We needed to. Too often financial professionals are under the impression that they have to talk slowly to give information to us women so we could grasp what they're saying. It seems that they are "talking down to us" and at a certain point in advance investment concepts and strategies terms get complicated, but is the job of a good financial professional to take complicated concepts and translated into real world terms. This book covers basics of everyday financial tips that will help you get really good control of yours finances. There is no shame in picking up this book, to learn what is not taught formally in school. After extended research, I discovered that there are no books that tell it like it is with realistic examples on how to manage your finances, at least the basic financial concepts. Basic financial education is something that you should be learning at home, the mathematical portion of finance it should've been learning in school, but unfortunately it is something that is basic and is overlooked; sometimes parents believe that the school system will teach their children about finances, and the school believes that is something they should be taught at home by the parents. Frankly, I believe that a lot of people learn to manage their money by watching their parents and by their own experiences. Talking about money is a taboo for some parents because they do not want to show their lack of control on the subject. Of course is not always the case since most people when it comes their finances, have been taught that by their parents in conjunction with school.

The level of control a woman has on her money has nothing to do with the amount of the formal education she has. I know many women with college education whose financial life is a disaster and in women who cannot read or write how a stronghold of their finances. Is my strong wish that you use the information that is provided to you in this book, I know it sounds cocky but I learned from my own painful financial experiences as well other women's painful lesson. I also learned from successful savvy women financial experiences. I have a strong sense of sisterhood because I was brought up on among women. You see, my mother used to own a beauty school that she ran out to our house. So most afternoons there was plenty of drama. The usual story was of a cheating husband or boyfriend, but that was not the part of the story that was interesting. It was the reason why women would not leave. Money. Most of this women could not leave the abusing party and because they had no control over the money. So, lesson 1, money equal freedom. As I got older I learn that educated women did not have the upper hand in their uneducated counter parts. It is true that women with education make more money; the fact does not guarantee that they know how to manage and preserve their earnings. The best advice has been from older women some with education other with no education but all with great expertise under their belts. I must confess that each time I have taken the advice from the older ladies that wore financial healthy, things when well and when I have not, I have gain my own tragedy experiences. I do not want you to learn to be financial healthy the hard way, because even if you gain a bad lesson it does not mean you learn how to fix the problem, it only means that next time you would do it a different way. Remember this, that people do not get smarter as they get older, if you are stupid young woman you will become a stupid old woman. I want the best for you. I want you to be as wealthy as you could be. My love and respect for you.

Chapter 1
Accept your reality!

It is what it is, begin where you are now, I know it sounds like a cliché but it is true. We will begin from this point. "Accept your reality" is a saying that I learned from my father, it is something he always said before he could begin to fix a problem or at least try to commence to correct any situation. First, we must know what we have to work with, what are our resources and from the point, we could start to change are the current situation. The reality is not good or bad; it is just the current condition. If you feel insecure or secure about the topic of money, then that is where you are. Money has no sex, it respects both men and women in the same way and it respects you back as you respect it. Your upbringing is the primary factor that shapes your money practices. Many women wished that they had training and guidance about money during their upbringing. Most women grew up in homes that either avoided discussion about money or had arguments about it. There's no question that you will make mistakes with your money but men make mistakes also. The only difference is that men make mistakes sooner in their life's than women, therefore they develop the experience on how to manage and invest their money quicker because they usually work earlier than women do, at a younger age. Another great ability man have is their high level of forgiven and tolerance with their money mistakes, and are able to overcome and forgive themselves and move forward: {This is something we'll talk about later on throughout the book} The only differences with men and women are that men just take action and learn from their experience. If men do well they boast about it and if they don't do well they forget about it and act like it never happened or blame the other party's fault in the transaction. Women need to act in the same way. So the point doesn't be so hard on

yourself learn all you can and about the purchase or transaction you want to take action on by asking professionals, and researching on the topic and always cross check your resources and most of all trust your gut, and then act! It is that simple. We women are very good asking questions to research so you should have no problem obtaining answers you seek. Money is just a tool for you to use, to get what you want. Men and women are scared to talk about money and gain control of their finances. You need to talk about your financial situation. The first step is to put it all on paper, to see what you have, what you owe and what you want.

This action is important because it will create a great relief in your psychic, and from that point, you could begin to ask the correct questions and develop a strategy. Your strategy should work because it designed for you. Be confident that your strategy will work because you can adjust it as you need it.

Chapter 2
Get organized

Getting organized is the best secret I learned from my mother and the most useful tool. It is very simple, doing so will make you feel good and be secure about your finances. The first thing you must do is write down a list of your debt, things you owe, all your debtors, and all the things you would like to get an own in the future. The method I use is a monthly planner.

The first step – In a piece of paper write down the amounts you owe, to whom, and the due dates.

Second step- Divide your bills into two sets; the ones that need to get pay the first half of the month and the second set of bills that needs to get pay the second half of the month.

Third step - Pick two specific dates in the month one at the beginning of the month (1-3) and another at the second half of the month (15-17) to pay your bills. It very important to make the payments on the same date each month, so you be able to write down all the

payments you made on the particular date, to whom and for how much as well as what bank account you used and the confirmation numbers this will be recorded in your planner. You would do the same process with the second date off the month you selected to pay the second set of bills that are due at the end of the month. The best method I use to pay the bills is online. I do not use automatic payments just in case I don't have the money. I make the payments manually for those particular dates I want to pay. Keep in mind that you could always try to change the due date on your bills to fit your money cycle. Avoid making payments over the phone, because most of the time there's a charge. If

ones that are due at the beginning month and the ones that are due on second half of the month. you use the mail, get your mail out with sufficient time, so bills arrive on time.

How to set-up your planner

Step One- In the very back pages of your planner write down the two sets of payments the

Below stepped below the line.

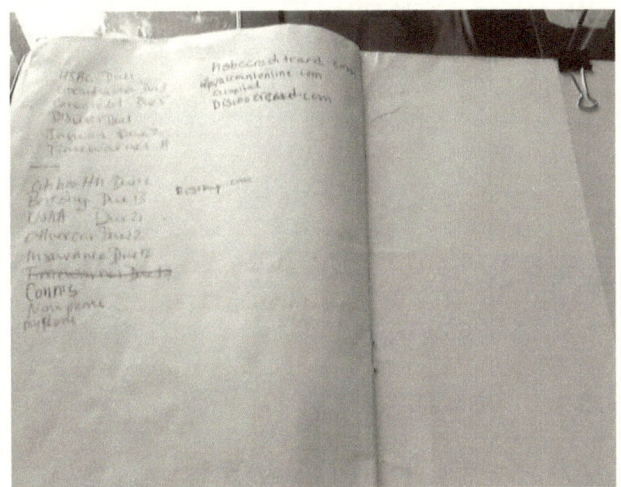

Example A: Name of the company you owe, due date and the amount.

Date from 1-14

Who You Owe	Due	Cost
Citibank	1	$25
Discovery	3	$20
Car payment	5	$350
Cable	5	$45

Date from 15-31

Citibank health card	15	$45
Master Card	18	$50
Insurance payment	19	$120
Gym	25	$178

Step two- On another page in the back of the

planner write down all the 1-800 numbers,

websites of each of your bill as well as login

name and password hint.

Example B:

web site

www.citihealthcard.com

Phone 1-800-455-5555

User Name   babyana

Pass word or hint My cat name

Account# 3455656

web site

www.discovercard.com

Phone 1-800-785-8585

User Name   babyana45

Pass word or hint My cat name

Account# 885541

Remember to keep the planner in a safe place. If you do not want to put your password, you could give yourself a hint that will let you remember. This system will keep your bills organized and keep them handy. Always keep the planner with you. The planner works wonderfully because you do not have to keep all the paper bills you receive in the mail and at the same time it gives you something tangible without the clutter. The planner also helps you keep track of all major expenses any time you might need to refer to them. Write down all important and non-important things that you might need to refer to in the future. The planner is currently like a ledger where you could have all the information at your fingertips. I know that there are all kinds of digital devices that you can use. Which don't require doing it "old-school", but believe me this is very simple and it doesn't take a lot of time and once you got it down it is something that you could use, to help you all the time and/or have in your home or office. Just remember to write things down and it will substantially remove all the clutter.

The planner comes handy because if you ever have a billing dispute and you know you have paid, you could easily go back to the planner and get the particular confirmation information. I keep all my planners and could easily go back to 10 years.

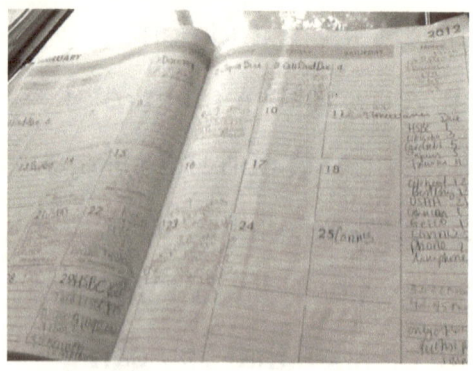

Chapter 3

Learn the financial rules

Learn the rules of the game. This is where you will become an investigator and your own best friend. For this section I want you to imagine that you are your best friend, you want to help her find the best school for her to enroll in. You would do that for your friend, right? I want you to use the same effort that you could use to help others to help yourself. You can begin slowly, but you have to keep moving. I will begin at the library by getting books on money management, once you get familiar with the lingo and build up your confidence you could, enroll in classes; keep in mind that is like learning another language so don't be too hard on yourself remember that people don't learn another language overnight. Do not be intimidated to dab into new information, if we all knew all the information we need it there would not be a need for school. Next, I would interview with a financial advisor, by phone or in person. Keep in mind that even though financial advisors are intimidating and you feel you don't know anything about investments. You are still the boss remember that without you using their services or buying their products they cannot make money. Please do not be rude to any of the professionals you talk too. They are also trying to make a living. Now what you have been waiting for, the mother-of-pearl, the golden grail, the core to financial health, what you must know to be financials healthy. You must, must, must lose the fear of asking questions, all types, all kinds, to anyone. This is one of the biggest hurdles you must overcome. Even though you might not get the answer from the first person you ask, sometimes because you did not word it correctly or you did not ask the correct person, or they did not have the answer, every time you ask a question you get closer to your answer and obtain clarity. This act alone is the single most important lesson my mother taught me and is the one lesson I want my daughters to remember and use every day of their lives. Don't let anyone make you feel ashamed or stupid for asking questions, because I tell you that it takes big ovaries to not be afraid. Asking the questions does not mean that you will act on all you hear. You take the information you can, then cross check from the different resources and finally make a decision without regrets. Learning the financial basics is the first step you take before you become a great investor. I believe you could not invest in the future if you can't control your money situation today. How much money you make? how do you get your money? and how much money you need to cover your basic needs and wants? Now, let's learn about checking, credit, insurance, and housing basics.

We will cover the essential basics topics, of course, there is always a vast amount of information on each, but this is just the basics.

Bank Account

Having a checking account is the number one thing you should do as soon as possible, it will help you establish financial existence in society. Your bank account is yours and yours alone the same as your credit history. A bank account is the number one thing you should have, even if you buy everything cash, you need to establish yourself with society. If you do not have a good bank account, you will have a hard time establishing a credit history. You need to have a checking account that is healthy and active so that means no bouncing checks and overdraft fees; now a day's creditors look to see if you had bank fees, to determine if you are able to manage your finances well. If you have joint accounts and you get a divorce, or become widowed the joint account may be closed. There are big differences between national banks and credit unions. I prefer credit union because they do not have so many fees. The only negative aspects of credit unions checking account are that they do not have branches everywhere, but they are good if you do not travel much. Note if you do travel make sure you have

plenty of cash in the account or you could use your regular credit cards and just pay what you would regular pay if you had your debit card. Understanding the Pre-printed Information on Your Checks .It is important to understand the information that is already printed on your checks so you can write checks accurately and completely. Below is a diagram of all the pieces of information you will find on a check:

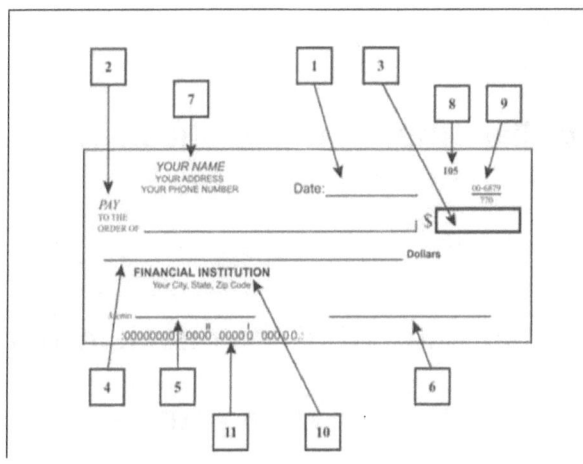

What You Will Need to Complete:

To complete your checks, you will need to fill in the following pieces of information:

1. The date.

2. The Pay to the Order of line.

This is where you write the name of the person or company to whom you will give the check. After writing the name, you can draw a line to the end. This prevents anyone from adding an additional name on your check.

3.The dollar amount of the check in numbers.

Such as $19.75.

4.The dollar amount of the check in words.

Such as 75/100. After writing out the amount of the check, draw a line to the end. This prevents anyone from adding an additional amount after what you have written.

5.section.

This area is optional. You can use this area to remind yourself why you wrote the check or to record the account number of the bill you are paying.

6.The signature line.

What is on the Check That You Will Need to Know:
7.Your name and address.

8.Your phone number is sometimes included.

9.The check number.

The number is used to identify each check written.

Codes for the state where the bank is located and the regional Federal Reserve Bank that will handle this check.

10.Your bank's number and branch.

11.Routing numbers.

This includes the bank and state computer routing numbers, as well as your account number.

What is On the Back of Your Check:

There is also important information printed on the back of your checks:

```
ENDORSE HERE

_____

_____

_____
DO NOT WRITE, STAMP OR SIGN BELOW THIS LINE
RESERVED FOR FINANCIAL ISTITUTION USE*
```

. The back of the check has **an endorsement area**. Endorsing a check means to sign the back of the check to make it "cashable." For example, if you write a check to your friend, your friend would endorse the check to get the cash or the deposit the amount into his or her account

Check Example

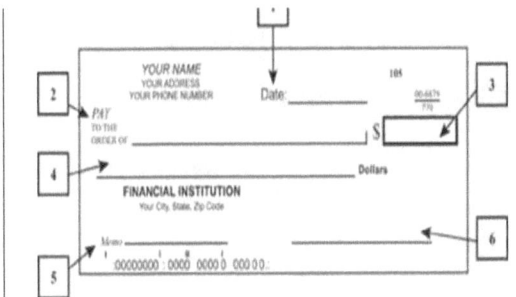

When writing a check, be sure to complete the following areas:

1.Date—Write the date.

2.Pay to the Order of—Write the name of the person or company to whom you will give the check. After writing the name, you can draw a line to the end. This prevents anyone from adding an additional name on your check.

3.$--Write the amount of the check in numbers, such as $19.75.

4.Dollars—Write the amount of the check in words, such as nineteen and 75/100. After writing out the amount of the check, draw a line to the end. This prevents anyone from adding an additional amount after what you have written.

5.Memo: This section is optional. You can use this area to remind yourself why you wrote the check or to record the account number of the bill you are paying.

6.Signature line: Sign your name.

A correctly filled out check will look like this:

YOUR NAME
YOUR ADDRESS
YOUR PHONE NUMBER   Date: __2/26__   105   90-6679/770

PAY TO THE ORDER OF __Coffee Mart__ $ [19.75]

__Nineteen and 75/100__ ————————— Dollars

FINANCIAL INSTITUTION
Your City, State, Zip Code

Memo __coffee maker__   __Your signature__

:00000000: 0000 00000 00000:

Consequences of Bouncing a Check
If you write a bad check...

1. Each bad check might cost you a fee of $10 to $30.

2. Additional checks you have written may not be paid.

3. Your negative activity can be reported to account verification companies like ChexSystems and TeleCheck. This can make it difficult to cash checks and to open accounts in the future.

4. Your bank also can close your account and send a negative report to the credit bureaus. The amount of the overdraft and fees might be reported as a collection item.

5. Some states have additional consequences. Writing a bad check is a crime in every state. Each state has different civil and criminal penalties. For example, some states have monetary penalties, such as $1,500 fine. Others may actually call for jail time and a fine. In some states, writing a bad check is a felony with imprisonment for up to five years.

Protect Yourself Against Writing Bad Checks

Not having the money in your checking account to pay the check you wrote is called an overdraft. Most banks offer overdraft protection, or bounce protection. This protects you from writing bad checks.

When you sign up for overdraft protection the bank will use the money from another one of your accounts to cover the transactions if you don't have enough money in your checking account.

Check your credit report

I personally believe you should pay in cash; in order not to pile credit debt, but you must learn to play the financial game in order to create the existence in the financial world. You must have credit available to you in case you should ever need it. You could start with a secure credit card that automatic report to the 3 major credit bureaus.

What is a secured Credit card?

A secured credit card is a credit card that will help you establish or re-establish your credit. A security deposit is generally required when you want to use this card. So, in essence the credit card companies are still lending you money but if you fail to pay off your bill in time, the credit card companies can deduct the money out of your deposit.

If you're looking to establish credit for the first time, these are good even if you pay an annual fee. It is ok. If you do not have credit and you apply for a regular credit card and you get deny, it will affect your credit score. That is why; secure cards are good because they eliminate the problem of being denied. Keep in mind that fees associated with these types of credit cards are a little higher than those of a regular credit card on the market. This is because as mentioned above, they are targeted toward people with bad credit o no credit. If you have no credit, companies are more hesitant to lend to you causing rates and fees to be a little bit higher.

How Does a Secured Credit Card Work?

A secured credit card is a little different than your regular credit cards. A secured credit card works almost like a prepaid credit card in a way. When you fill out your application and get approved, you will want to send in a deposit to the bank. The bank is asking for a deposit because if you don't pay off your bill in time, the bank will have collateral to work with. This means that if you don't pay your bill, the bank can take money out of your deposit account. If you're looking for a credit card to make purchases online or at the store, this card will work just like a credit card. All major credit card companies such as Visa and MasterCard carry these types of cards.

The only thing different is when you make your payment to the companies themselves. As for making purchases in the store, nothing will change on that end. A security deposit is needed by a bank because as mentioned above, the card holder probably doesn't have enough credit or their credit history is bad. If a bank has a deposit, this means that they won't have to worry about the cardholder not paying their bill off in time. If the cardholder doesn't pay their bill, they can simply deduct the payments from the

Capital One Secured Master Card

http://www.capitalone.com/credit-cards/secured-mastercard/

1-800-227-4825

Applied Bank, Secured Visa Gold Credit Card

https://www.applefcu.org/CreditCards/Platinum#tab6

707-788-4800

security deposit. Remember, if you continue to not pay off your bill on time,

you won't be able to establish your credit. These are some of the ones I like.

Check all fees before you get a secure card. Once you get them you must use the cards correctly and pay them on time for about a period of one year. After a year you could request to have you credit line increase, the amount that I suggest to charge should be $25 and then pay off the $25 in full each month. You should do this for about 3 months; you could pay for what you regular pay in cash such as gas, and etc. This can be done at the beginning when you are establishing a credit history. The point is to get credit and then use it, as to establish usage history. Once you have an established credit history, I advise you to just get only larger purchase on credit since you should never charge everyday expenditures because you will be paying high-interest rates. Sometimes at the beginning of your credit history, you get higher interest rate and that is ok because the amount you use will be paid in full and once credit is established you then could request a better credit rate. Remember if you are just the authorized–user it does not mean you are the owner of the account or getting the benefit of the credit company reporting to the credit bureaus.

Credit Reporting and Agencies

Equifax

Equifax, Inc.

Disclosure Department

P.O. Box 740241

Atlanta, Georgia 30374

Experian

PO BOX 2002

Allen, TX 75013

1-888-397-3742

Trans Union

PO BOX 1000

Chester, PA 19022

1-800-888-4213

Buying a phone

If you are going to buy a phone you should get
a no contract month-to-month phone
company. It is not worth to get in a contract
and getting your credit damage
because you do not have the money to pay for
one month. A phone bill could prevent you
from getting really important things in life like a
house and a car. You could get a nice phone
you could flash to your phone carrier. Do
not get landline or an actual house phone,
there are too many fees associated to them/ is
just not worth the amount you will pay per
month.

Buying a car

"My experience on buying a car. When I purchased my first car it was a brand new Nissan Sentra and I was 23 years old. I went to the dealer who got me a loan for 21% for 5 years with $2000 cash down. My payments wore $450 per month, it was crazy! Anyway I got the car reposes twice, but I did pay off the car in full after 6 years. I did not know how to buy a car, because nobody taught me the correct way of buying a new car and I learned the hard way. My father who was the official car purchaser,

was terrible at it, when it came time to negotiate he would scream at the salesman would and get so emotional. He

never trust the salesman. When I bought my first new car is when I realized my father had never bought a new car. He only ever purchased used cars. I later realized that he used those tactics of screaming and yelling to Intimidate the seller, at the time it was terrible embarrassing for me. This is not to put my father down. Now that I'm an adult I understand the reason that he only buys used cars was because he didn't want to be in debt. Now I will teach you how to buy a car the correct way. Begin by deciding what you could pay for month, the total amount of the car the car and the type of vehicle and

model you want. Then you look at different dealership websites online to determine the average price for the car you want. Lesson one: Never buy the current year model or new model, you should only buy one year used because you pay more. Secondly, you go to a credit union or bank and get an estimate of how much you could borrow and what you interest rate would be. Third, do not

give your social security number to the car

dealership they will try to tell you they could get you a better rate and some time is true but they will add all kinds of stuff and charge you don't need, such as extend warranties etc. When you find the car you like, get what is call **Vehicle Identification Number.** Give this number to your credit
union or bank. You could just call you credit union or bank. If the salesperson those does not want to give you the vehicle identification number, most likely a car is not
worth the amount they want. That is why salesperson usually asks you to put money down. The money you put down is the difference of the car is worth. Many banks and credit unions will not ask for your money down. If the car you're purchasing is worth more than the amount you're paying for it according to the Kelly blue book. Of course, it depends on your credit scores and history.

You credit union or bank will also ask you the year and a model of car. Before you sing anything you will then ask the banker if the car is worth what the dealer price is asking. Remember to borrow enough money to cover registration and plates.

 Then you will go to the dealer and they will give you a purchase order and you will take that to your bank. All you have to do is pick the paperwork on the car and the bank will wire the money to the dealer. I have bought many cars since my first new Nissan with a nice low-interest rate.

Auto Insurance

Your insurance rate is based on what you do for work, how many miles you drive and what type of car you drive more expensive cars and sports car gets charged more. Insurance is almost always more expensive for men than women. Confused about insurance, don't be. The law requires you to carry insurance on your person in case you are involved in car wrecks, housing problems, body injuries, etc. This is called Liability- this is divided into two parts; the car part (property damage) and body part (bodily injury). The state set the minimum you have to have in each and this is the minimum insurance you could have, it does not protect you or your car at all and you could have this type if you haven't financed your car. If you finance your car, then you need insurance that

protects your car as well all collisions,

comprehensive you could also buy medical coverage for your medical expenses. The uninsured motorist pays for your car's damages when the other person hit you isn't able to pay enough insurance or no insurance at all. There are financial limits with each coverage and you do not have an endless amount of money to protect you. Also, it's good to keep in mind that just because your state may not require extensive insurance, extra coverage may be worth the expense. After all, no one wants to be stuck with thousands of dollars in bills because of an auto wreck. My rule of for insurance is, "the more you have to lose, the more insurance you should have." There is more type of insurance, such as life, health, and property but we will discuss this in the future.

compare the best rate. I like Allstate but you could buy online http://www.renterlife.com or 1-877-574-7280

Rental Insurance

This is what you need to know, if you are renting a room, apartment or house. You need rental insurance it only cost a few dollars some start at $8 and up off course it dependent what you own. Rental insurance is very affordable and it will help you replace your personal things. Depending upon the specifics of your policy, renter's insurance will replace or repair property that has been stolen or damaged, provide emergency lodging, or pay legal fees. A building owner is not responsible for a renter's personal property, legal liability to others within the premises, accidental injury or property damage that might arise within your premises or from your personal actions. Ask you could call around a few company to

Condominium Insurance

This is people how leave in a condominium complex it cover you unite. There is additional coverage used for the community part of the complex and to cover liability.

The condominium owner has a deed to private living space, plus "common areas," like entrances, clubhouses, pools, and the like, that are frequented by all condominium owners and their guests. In a building with eight apartments, you hold a deed on an apartment and, according to the provisions of the deed, are the owner of the apartment plus a designated share of the public areas. The building personified as the condominium association is an entity with power to manage, buy and sell individual units within the building, as well as maintain and manage the property that encompasses the building into an entity. Condominium owners have unique insurance requirements covered only by an insurance policy specifically designed for condominium living. Condominium insurance provides coverage for the owner's personal possessions, improvements to the an interior of the unit, and legal liability for injury or damage suffered by visitors. Coverage of the building is usually the responsibility of the condominium association. A condo owner may incur added responsibility for common areas like lobbies, hallways and recreational facilities, and legal liability for a visitor injured there if the condominium association coverage proves inadequate. A careful review of the condominium association's proprietary lease will reveal the structural parts of the building already covered. Some associations are responsible only for bare essentials, such as walls, floor, and ceiling, and the owner is required to ensure interior decorations, plumbing, dishwasher, dryer, wiring fixtures, etc.

Life Insurance

I like this one if you have people how depend on you. The most affordable on is Term Insurance. You pay a set amount each month per a set amount your family will get if you do die in the set amount you selected.

The are many type of insurance out there to protect most all things, but this are just the basic. You should ask an insurance agent to point out to you all your need that you may not be able to see.

Real Estate

Housing is my favorite topic! We all have to live somewhere. I can totally get **Scarlett O'Hara,** this girl got the idea of housing importance. Women are so affected by this topic since the housing budget takes up more of the income. I am always surprised on how many women do not know anything about their housing.

They always leave this decision to the men in their life. I was that type of woman once. My first housing purchase was the fantasy of every first time female buyer. I was 23 with one child and pregnant with my second baby. My first home purchase was with VA loan, it was a new construction $165,000 house I did not know or cared to much about the transaction itself all I cared about was that my husband told me that we could afford it and I

believed him. The first time I became aware that I needed to learn about real estate was when the lender required me to sign a quick claim on the property, mean quick rights on the house. At that point I felt deceived and stupid, but I want a house for my children so I sing. I lived there for several years and one day we began getting default letter in the mail explaining that we were behind
on the mortgage and that we could possibly lose our house. That is when I took charge of the real estate situation for the first time and hired a dynamic real estate broker to help sell my house before things got out control
and my profit doubled the price of the house. And in that moment when the light bulb in my head lit up, I decided to learn about real estate and payoff my house in full as
soon as possible. I would not leave in fear that

someone would kick me or my children out and I became the landlord.

Now when I say I am a house owner it means I own the entire place in full. Big mistake everyone in the household should know the housing situation even if they are not the ones that pay the bills. For the most part men take out the lease on their name so women don't get to develop credit housing history. The only time that I have seem a woman give the lease on their name is when the husband or spouse has poor credit. I am not stereotype I see in this, now a day many women buy, rent or lease under their own name and good for them! All I could tell you is that you need to have a way of knowing that if you need to get your own place you could do that for yourself.

Buy properties before you could buy you have to have for the most part rental history, credit and most important an income. Many women have two out of three but usually the most important are income. Of course, if you buy cash you do not need any of this. Once you have your place whether you buy or rent make sure you are aware of the activity in your accounts to make sure thing are being paid for on time. Many women sometimes do not have an idea if the husband pays on time, late or not at all. For more information, read my other book 'Could this be your next move". P.S. if you rent, buy renter insurance is not very expensive, it covers your personal items, and if you own buy property insurance, shop around not two companies are like. You should also know that if you have poor credit it could also affect your insurance rates.

Student Loans

Don't go crazy with the student and think that you will find a job and be able to pay your loan. Education does not always mean lot of money. One thing is to make money and another to have an education. When I was young the first skill I learn was cosmetology like my mother. From high school I when to cosmetology course and then to the shop, I was young and obedient and since I did not have a defiant plan to study I did what my parents toll me and I am glad I did. After I graduated I continue to go school and I would finance my education with the money I made at the shop. I at 19 years of old I was making $300 a day.

While my friend wore having add job and making mini wage. I realize that it was manual labor but it paid well.

Only when I got to the end of my college was when I got a student loan, because I could work as much because I was pregnant and want to finish. And let me tell you what happen once I graduated I was not making $300 like a did in the shop I did want to work in the shop because I want to be intellectual and guesses what I had knowable and no money. I no longer want to be in the shop because I got tire more easily. The point is that intellect does not equal a fat purse. Now do not get me wrong I paid $5000 for the course so I did make investment and study for one year. You could get an education study and work so you do not have to get a loan. P.S. my parent did not pay for my college all do my dad did pay the first $5000.

Tax

Do you need to file a federal tax return? Well according to the IRS, many individuals who do need to file tax returns still do, because don't know the requirements. You first need to at your gross income, this is your total personal income before taking taxes out. You could check www.IRS.gov , 1-800-829-1040. You could use www.vitasa.org to find a Vita site near you or call 1-800-906-9887 The VITA Program is IRS-sponsored Volunteer Income Tax Assistance. IRS-certified volunteers provide free basic income tax return preparation to qualified individuals in local communities. Even if you are self-employed but do not have any other worker other than you. They could guide you in the correct direction. Tax season begins January 1 and is due April 17. Please do not go to those places that give you your money right away without having to wait for your tax returns. You are paying around $300 in order to get your money without waiting. It's better to wait for your tax return and not lose so much money.

Buying Stuff Rent to Own

My advice juts don't buy anything rent to own. If you need to buy appliances pay cash, store credit like Sear, or use your credit card, but do not go to does place that tells you buy here and pay her.

They often over price the merchandise because they think you can't get credit somewhere else.

As for another item you want to buy, always compare how many things cost new and used before you buy. Please do not buy and get in debt with clothes, food, and gas, those things you should pay cash for.

I can't tell you the ridicules Victoria bill I have seeing, your breast will not be any different, they will just look better. You better just save the money and get plastic surgery.

Chapter 4

Get an Income

One of the most important life financial lessons to learn is to manage your money as soon as possible; equally, as importance is to learn to earn your money. When you earn your own money, you have a greater respect for it and for yourself. It becomes more than a numbers game. It is easy to make payments with other people's money. It is very different when it is your money and you are aware of how much each dollar costs you to earn. You must know what the market is willing to pay you for the type of work you do. Know what is your trade value in the workforce. You are only worth what people are willing to pay for your skill. When you enter the workforce you would learn quickly what type skills, education and/or experiences you need to make the money you would like to make. Women do not value their work as much as man values theirs. Men usually negotiate a better salary up front or they do not take the job, and I they can't more money they try to get job perks. We all have to begin somewhere. If you have no experience, education or skill, take whatever opportunity you can get. You could always get a better job when you gain the experience. I have

heard so many women that say, "no I will not take a job that pays me $7.50 because that is too little, I am fine, my husband make money for both of us." The first thing you must know is that if your husband goes so does the money. You do not have to take the job if you are doing something better with your life, such as going to school or learning something new. Whatever salary is offered to you is what you are worth according to society. Many women take the excuse that they can't work because they are taking care of their children, but that is no excuse.

If you want to study you could make it happen. It is sad to see how many women lose their comfortable lifestyle and is forced to go into the workforce do to a lost their husband's financial support do to a spousal sickness, divorce or death. If you think is frustrating to get paid $7.50 per hour when you are young, is not any better when you get older and you do not have the energy or your looks. If you are a poor girl, you will be a poor woman when you get older. With income come confidence and it removes shame.

Too many women's egos are hurt when they have to ask their spouse for money. We all have to start somewhere, is true that men have the upper hand because they never have to stop to take care of the children. You have to consider it a loss of time. If you are learning something you are still, consider having value in the marketplace.

You are still learning you are still in the game. Get an income through a job, your business, buy or selling, anything to create income. I cannot tell you the amount of women who have to destroy many of my business deals because they did not have a clue what was happy the marketplace. Many of these women have never worked a day in their lives and have no idea how are hard it is to earn a dollar. Many women set unrealistic expectation on their spouse. Don't expect a spouse, family or the government to take care of you, take care of yourself. I want to mention that my aunt Vicki and my mother have always been hard working women, I'm so proud of them.

Chapter 5

Lear to share your wealth!

This is a personal view, but I can't give you the incomplete formula. I give "El Shaddai" 10% from my earnings. Every time I get paid I give my tie. Personally, I give my tie where I get nurture spiritually. A do not pay much attention what the recipients do with the money. I know what is a mandate of me through the Torah and just do it. I also help any other way I can. I give the money because I do not always have the time or energy to volunteer. I think, that volunteering helps you develop the production mussel. When you begin to volunteer and try to help others, one quickly relies upon that you need more money and time.

I know that for me it creates a sense of urgency to want to make more money to share with others.

It also feels good to take care of others, and know that no one has to take care of you. Tiding is a sure formula for prosperity. The God of the universe want to be your LORD and he will make sure that you are the head, not the tail. Deuteronomy 28:13. Be a good world-class citizen and contribute to your wealth!

Chapter 6

Invest in Yourself

One of the longest-lasting investments you can make, with the best returns over time, is in yourself. Investing in yourself can help you improve your earning power, as well as provide you with a sense of satisfaction. Your knowledge and skills could not be taken away from you. The more skill you obtain the easier your life will get and the more choices you will have. As you learn more, the fear of the unknown will be less. You should try to learn a skill or gain knowledge before you need it. It's a form of loving yourself. You be surprised to see how many women sabotage them self. Keep in mind that there are many forms of learning, that not everyone learns the traditional way. Nowadays is easy to find many learning platforms. Engage in activities outside your comfort zone, join a community or student organization and travel to the new place. My mother was a fast learner. She would listen to conversations at work. She then would remember the conversations that were interesting to her and then research later in the subject she heard. My mother came to America when she was 34 years old and did not speak English. I learned to ask questions and research information from my mother.

If you are in the age of bringing your children, then you should be studying something. Remember that society will not have compassion or understand you. Maybe other mothers would have compassion for you, but there are many women who never had or will have children and they see things very different.

Do not cheat yourself out of the opportunity to stay marketable. You will be a more balanced human being with investing there are no guarantees, it does not matter if you are a man or a woman. It is true that there is no guarantee that higher education will bare all you higher income this day. One thing is for sure, that you will be a better human for having more education. You definitely won't feel any less when you compare yourself to a man. Please, before you enroll yourself in any school researchers the field. You research by going to your local unemployment office and see if the jobs are truly in demand. Don't just let the school you are enrolling into, tell you that you will find a job, but actually look up at the jobs that are viable for whatever you are studying.

In conclusion

When you begin to learn about money and hiring a money advisor, you should be aware that they are not your friends. Their business is to make money with yours; so you should have at least two advisors that you could cross check information and see who you feel more comfortable with.

When men make a purchase decision, large or small, they make their own decisions. Women do not make their own decisions; we women like to consult with others. The solution to this problem begins by making a small decision on your own. For the larger decision, research the best you can and then just do it! Remember that whatever you buy, you will be the one who will pay. Make a decision that you would want for yourself. If you let other people influence your decision you will still have fear of a new purchase, which is normal but since is not your complete choice you may end up paying for stuff you did not even like, need, or want. Advice, before you buy anything, ask others, research by asking an expert on the things you want to buy, read for yourself, do not be embarrassed to ask, and once you get the answer never jump ahead to make a move without crosschecking. Once you do that then make your decision with confidence. I am not saying to take a long time to make a decision, but after researching you would be ready to make a deal or quick decision when you find a good opportunity. So accept your reality, get organize, learn the laws of money, get or create an income, share your wealth and invest in yourself. And most importantly do all this with kindness.

Appendix A
References
Allstate
Appleid One Bank
Bible
Capital one
IRS
Orchard Bank

Ariana C P Hunter

Other Books @ Amazon, Barnes & Nobel

Are you at foreclosure street & rental avenue?

Could this be your next move?

Sesiòn Breve de Hipnosis

www.ingramcontent.com/pod-product-compliance
Lightning Source LLC
Chambersburg PA
CBHW030727180526
45157CB00008BA/3077